Dedicated to Niki, Dimitris, Lelis - Charikleia

Dedicated to my wonderfully patient husband and
Dora and her family, our parents - Elisavet

Copyright © 2020 Elisavet Arkolaki, Charikleia Arkolaki

Translated into Italian by Tiziana Fiorito

All rights reserved.

No part of this work may be reproduced, stored in a retrieval system, or submitted in any form or by any means, electronic, mechanical, photocopying, recording or otherwise, without the prior written per-mission of the publisher, except in the case of brief quotations embodied in critical reviews and certain other non-commercial uses permitted by copyright law. This book may not be lent, resold, hired out or otherwise disposed of by way of trade in any form of binding or cover other than that in which it is published, without the prior written consent of the publisher. Custom editions can be created for special purposes.

For permission requests and supplementary teaching material, please write to the publisher at liza@maltamum.com www.maltamum.com

ISBN 9798676720643

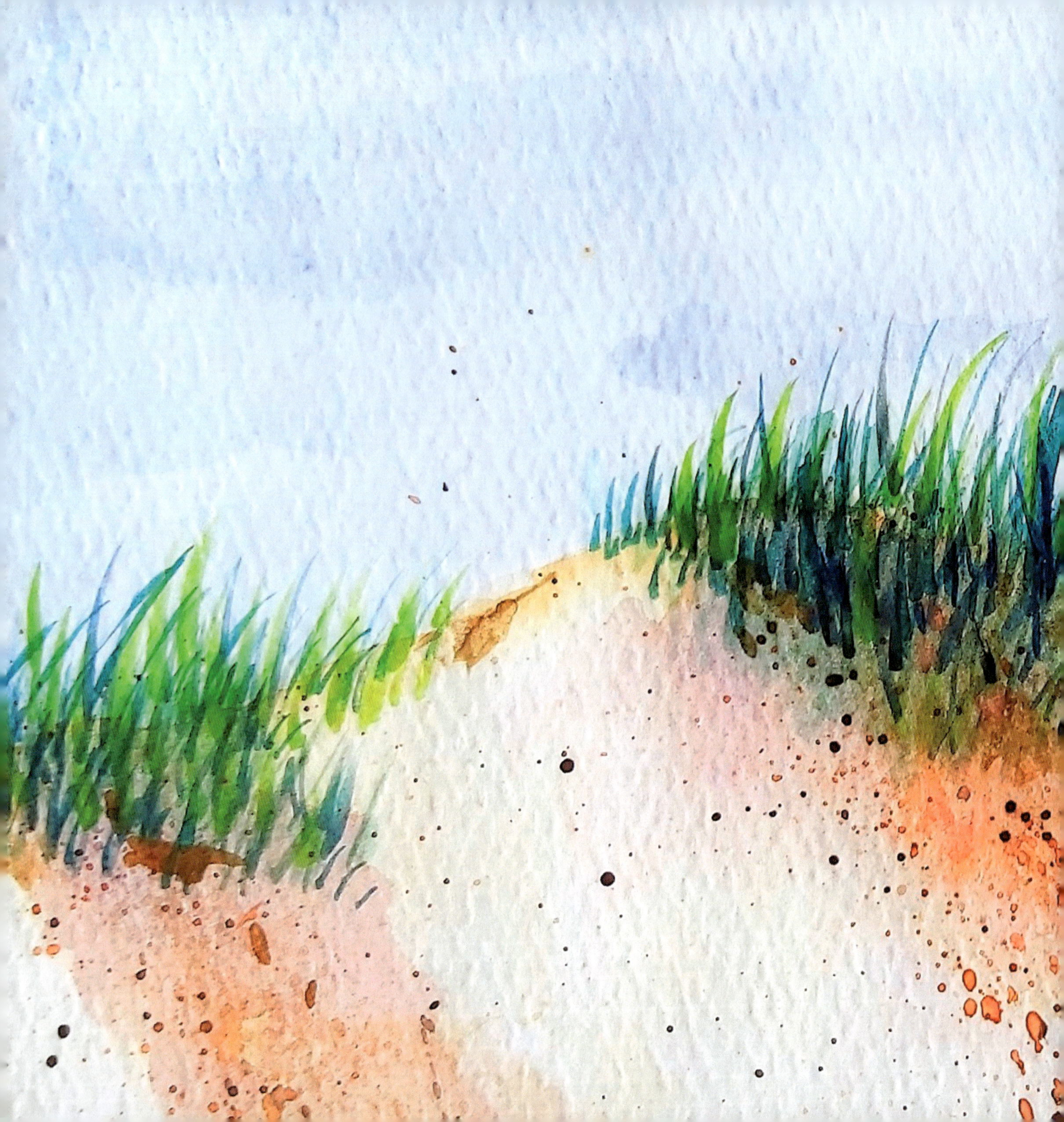

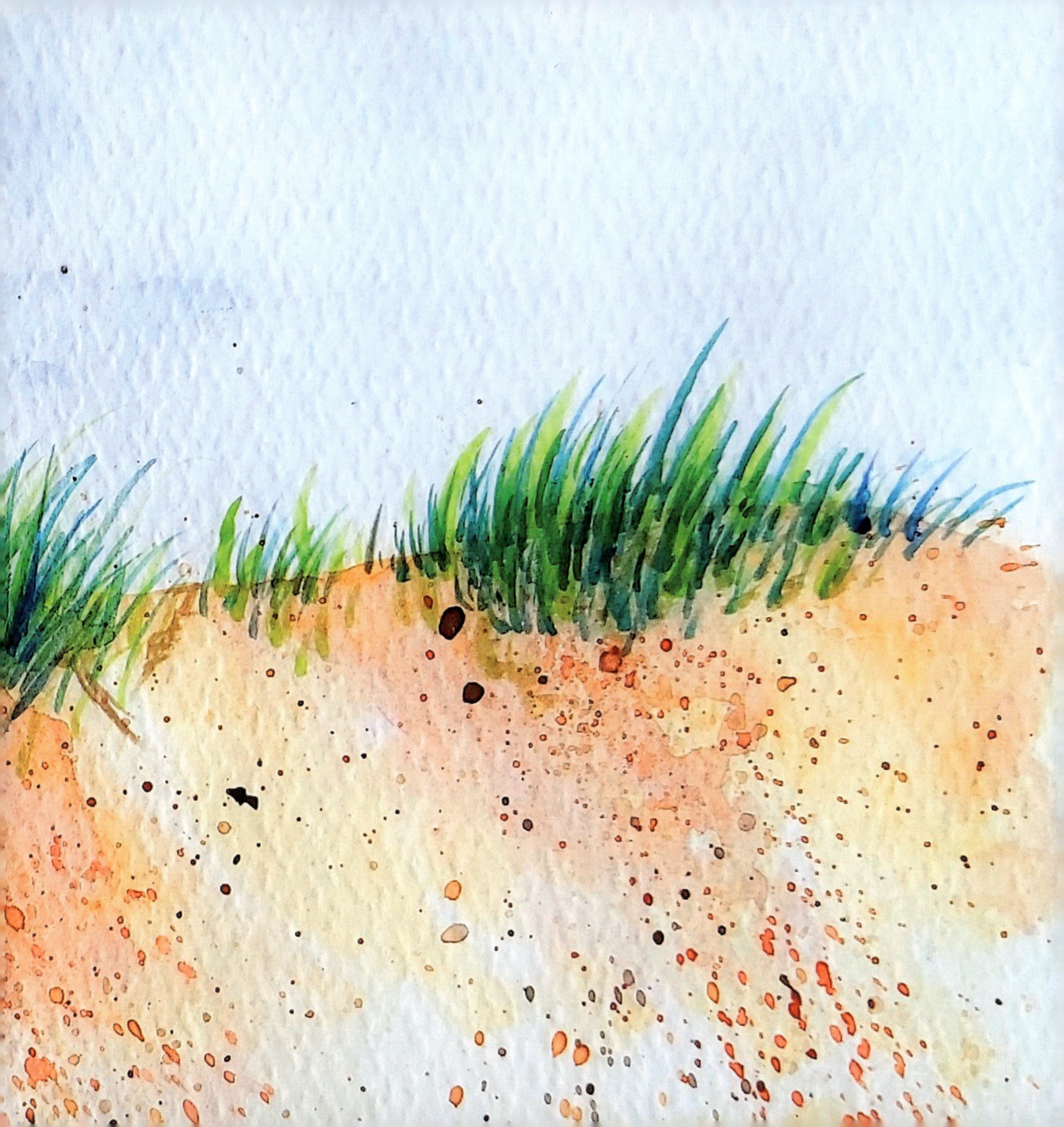

Today I felt like painting the sea. We took our brushes, watercolors, art pads, and a glass of water and sat on the veranda to paint. A little blue, a little yellow, a little brown and look, that's how it all started.

Oggi mi è venuta voglia di dipingere il mare. Abbiamo preso pennelli, acquerelli, blocchi da disegno, un bicchiere d'acqua, e ci siamo sedute sulla veranda a dipingere. Un po' di blu, un po' di giallo, un po' di marrone e, guarda, è così che è cominciato tutto.

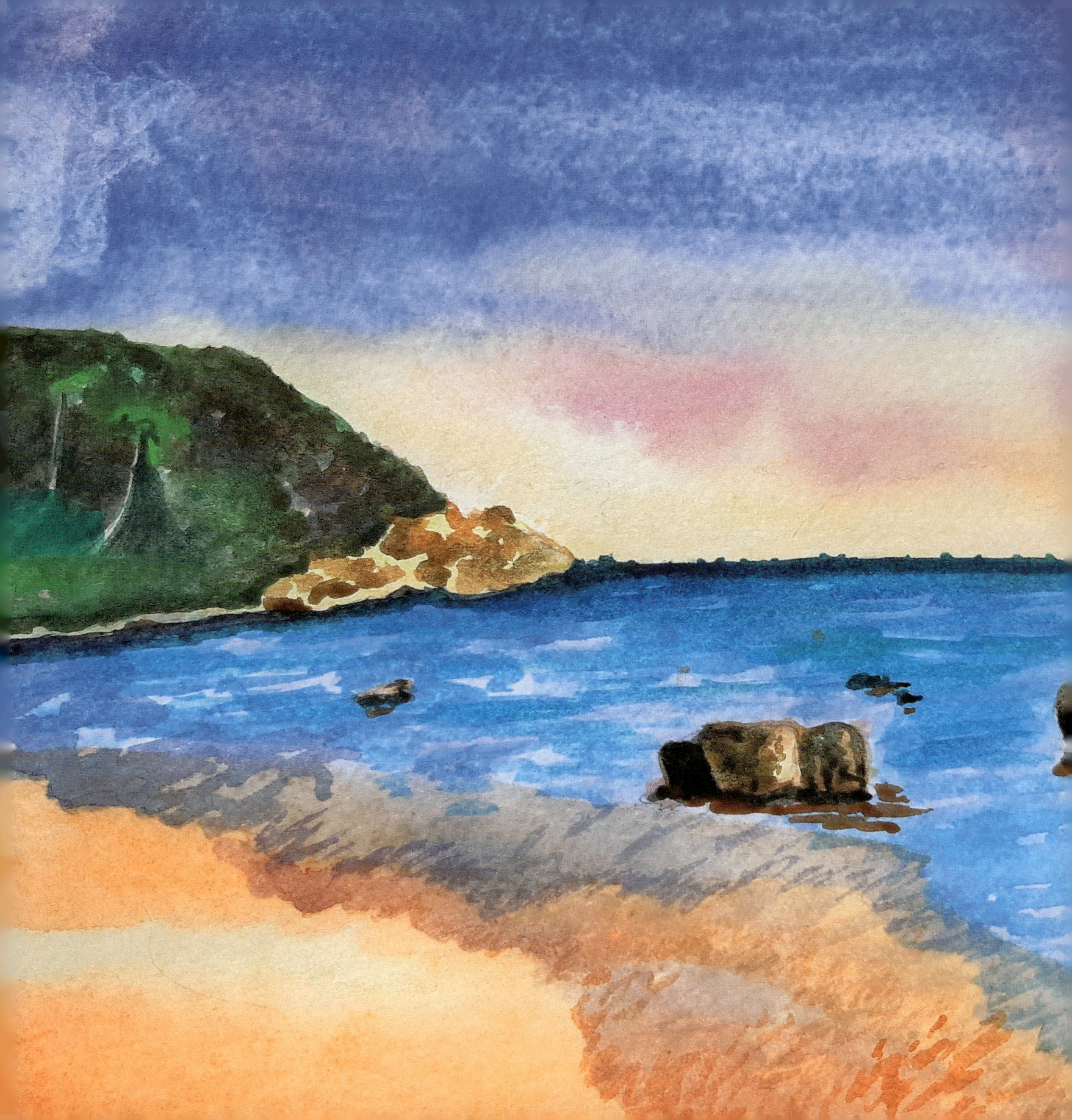

I was reminded of the summer vacations we took, to the place where my mother grew up, and I added some rocks to the landscape. Purple for sparse clouds and this green for the hill seem to be a great match.

Mi sono tornate in mente le vacanze estive che trascorremmo dov'era cresciuta la mamma, e ho aggiunto delle rocce al paesaggio. Il viola per Le nuvole sparse e questo verde per la collina sembrano un bell'accostamento.

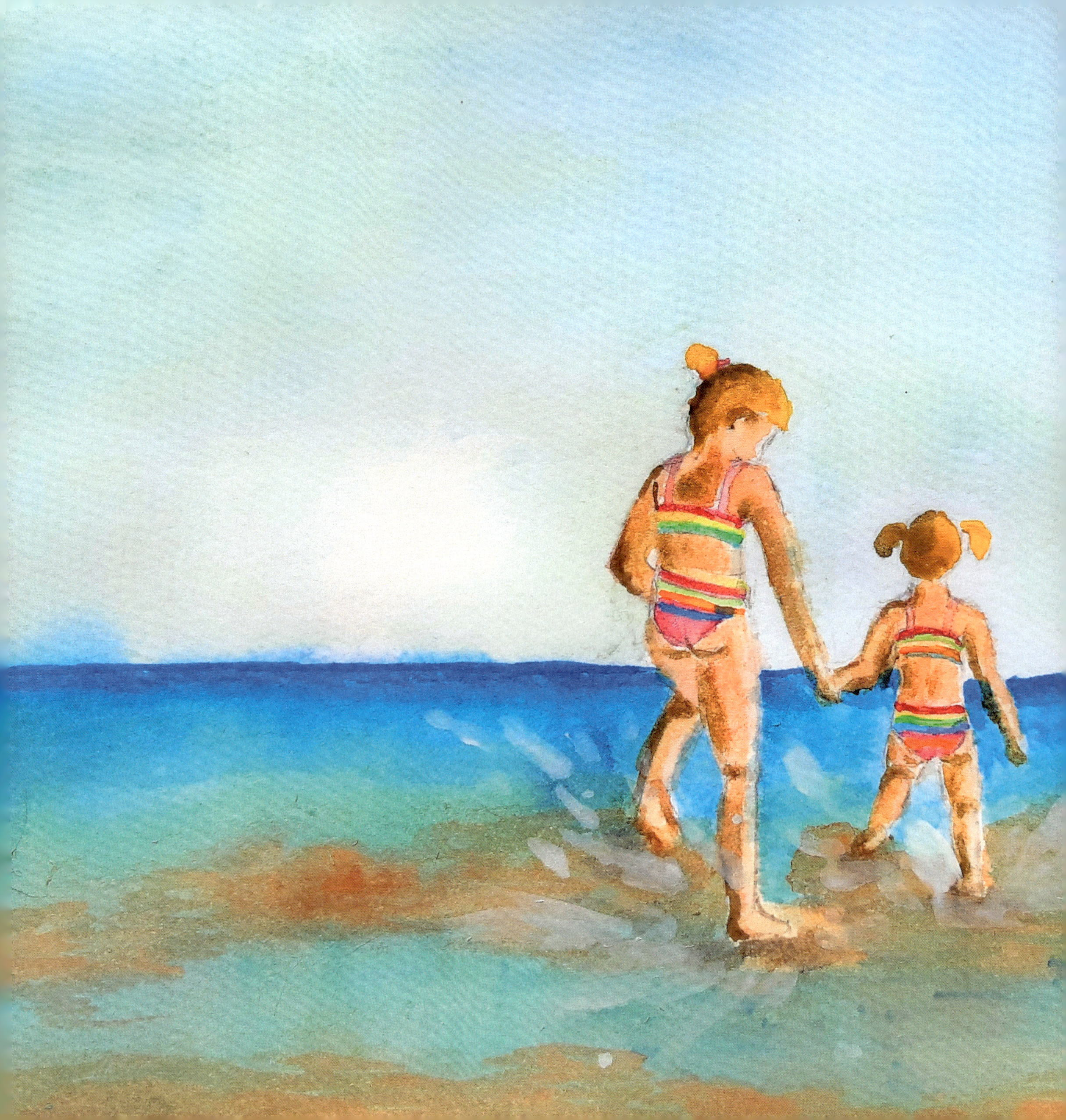

We'd go to the sea every morning and play there for hours. All the colors of summer were imprinted on our swimsuits. Intense yellow, intense blue, and intense orange.

Andavamo al mare ogni mattina e giocavamo per ore e ore. Tutti i colori dell'estate erano stampati sui nostri costumi: giallo intenso, blu intenso e arancione intenso.

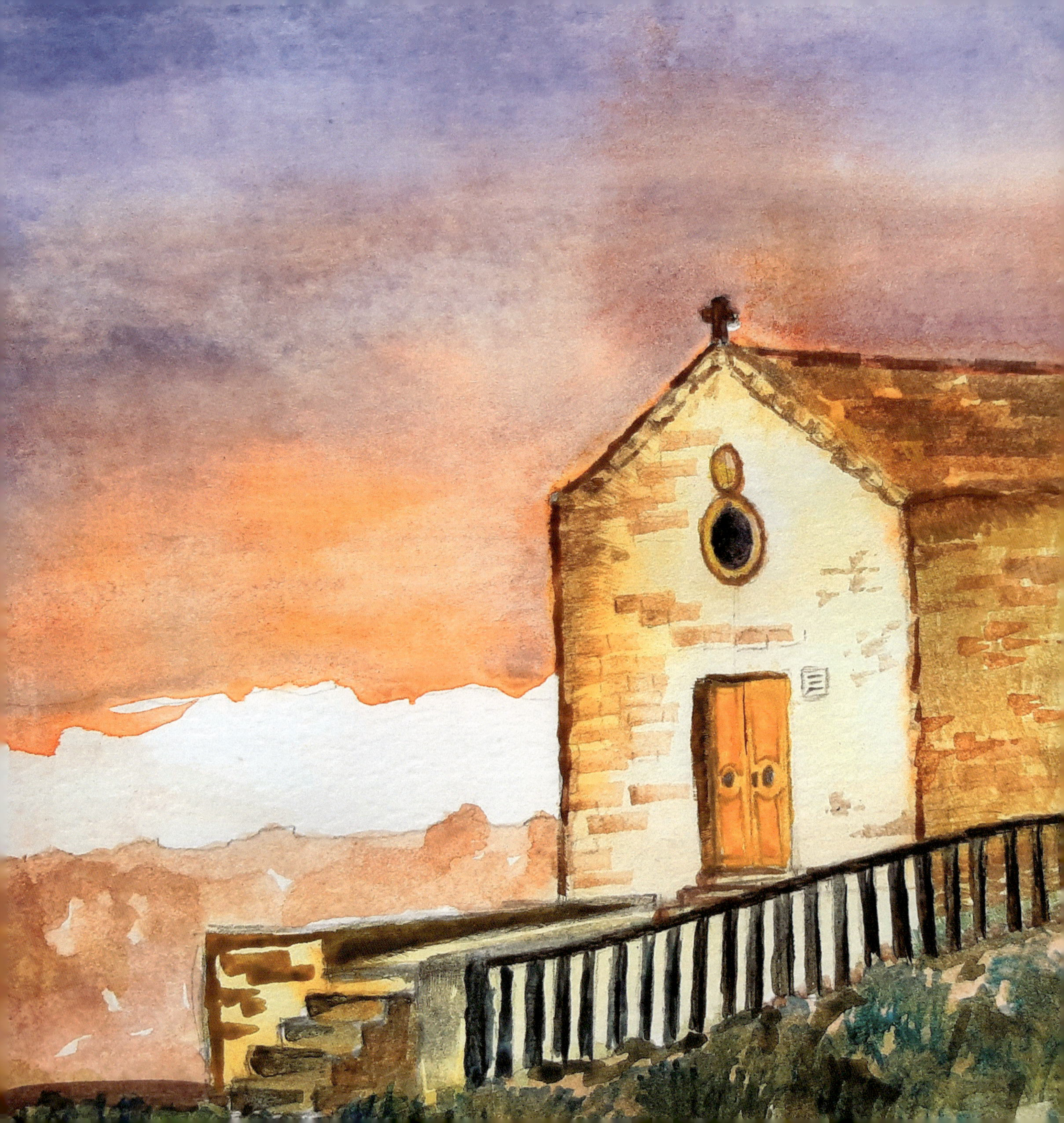

I also remembered the small church. It was on the hill. Our grandmother would sometimes take us there before we returned home for lunch. I'll mix a little brown, a little yellow, and a little green.

Mi venne anche in mente la chiesetta. Era sulla collina. La nonna ci portava lì qualche volta, prima di ritornare a casa per pranzare. Mescolerò un po' di marrone, un po' di giallo e un po' di verde.

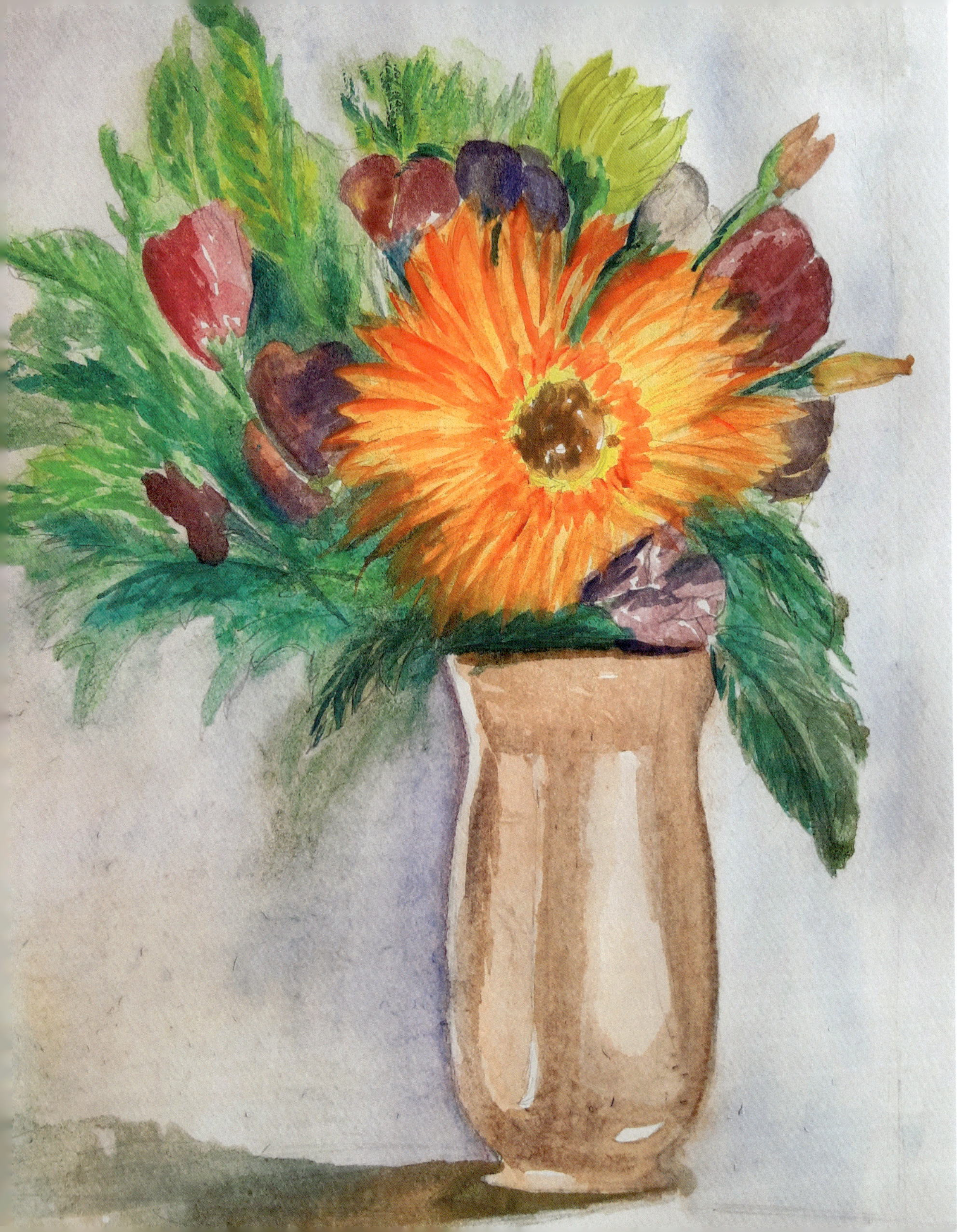

On the way back we often picked wildflowers to arrange them in a vase. I think orange, purple and green are very suitable here.

Sulla via del ritorno, spesso raccoglievamo fiori selvatici per poi metterli in un vaso. Credo che arancione, viola e verde qui ci stiano d'incanto.

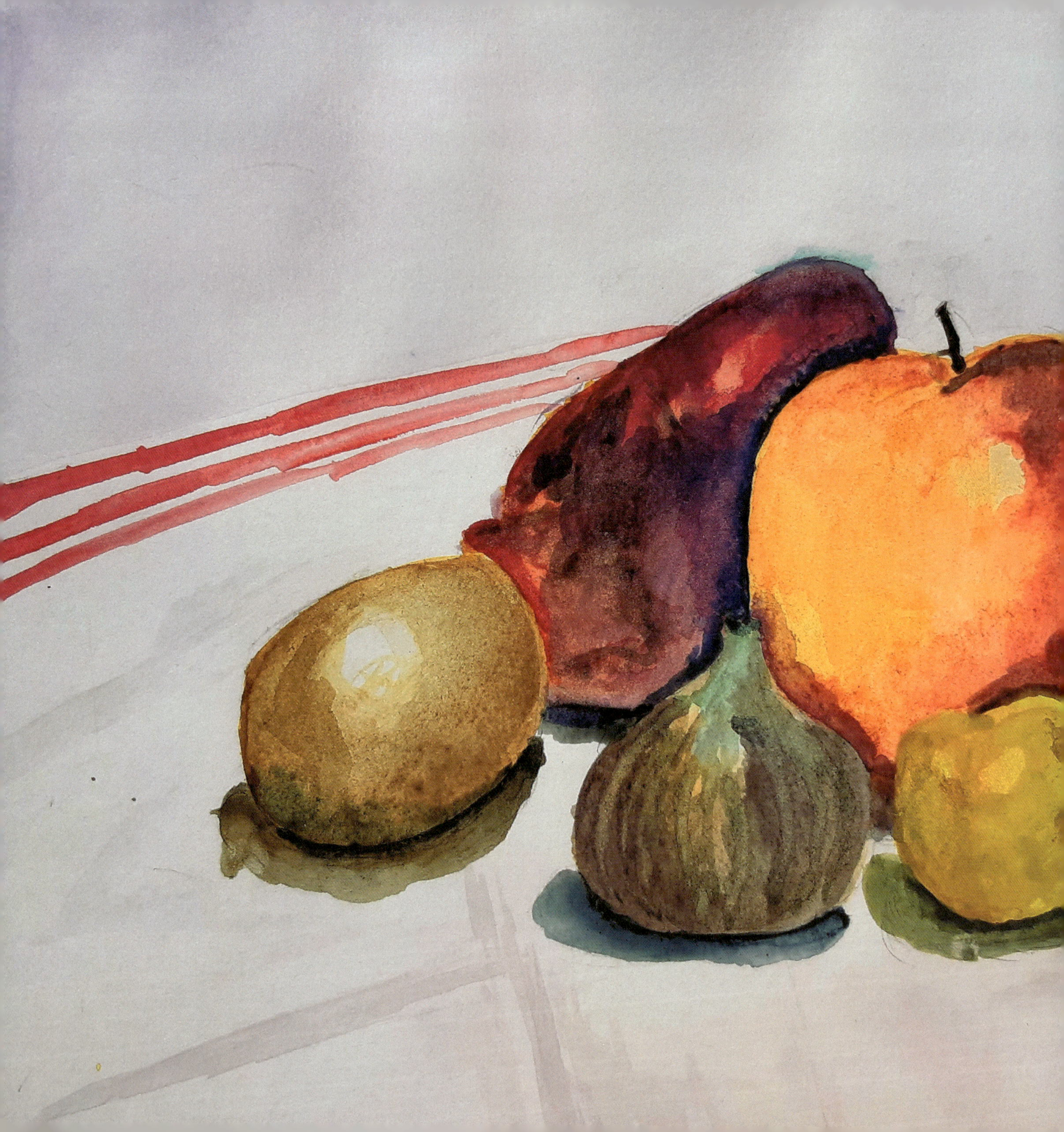

When we got home, and after we had eaten our food, she offered us the most delicious fruit. Green for the fig, orange for the apricot, and red for the peach.

Quando giungevamo a casa, dopo aver finito di pranzare, la nonna ci offriva la frutta più deliziosa. Verde per il fico, arancione per l'albicocca e rosso per la pesca.

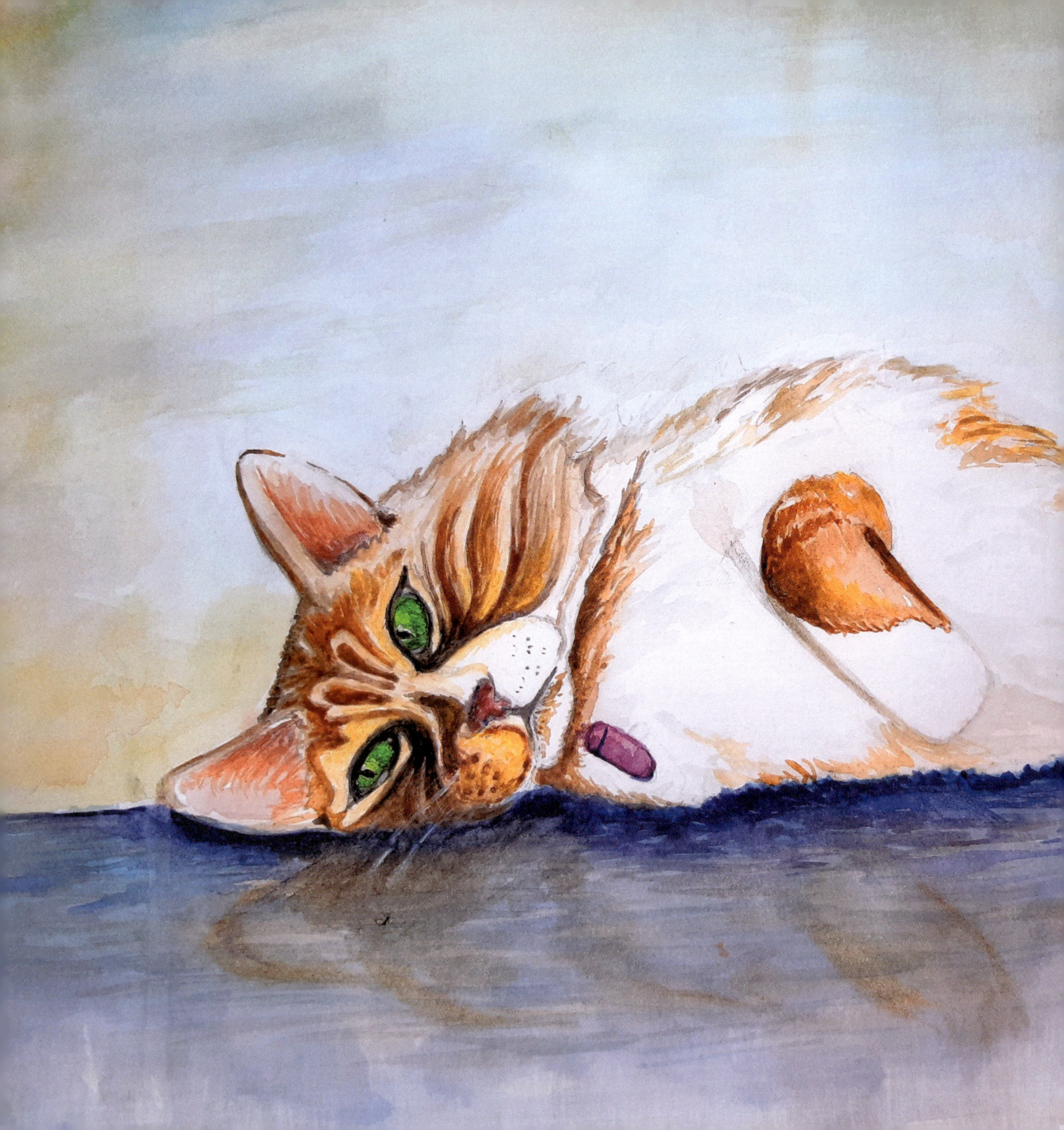

Grandma also had a cat. We played so many different games inside and outside, running after her in the narrow dead-end street. It was, indeed, Happiness Street! Her colors were white, brown, and bright green.

La nonna aveva anche una gatta. Facevamo così tanti giochi con lei, fuori e dentro casa, correndole dietro nella stradina stretta e senza sbocco. Era veramente la Via della Felicità! I colori della gatta erano bianco, marrone e verde brillante.

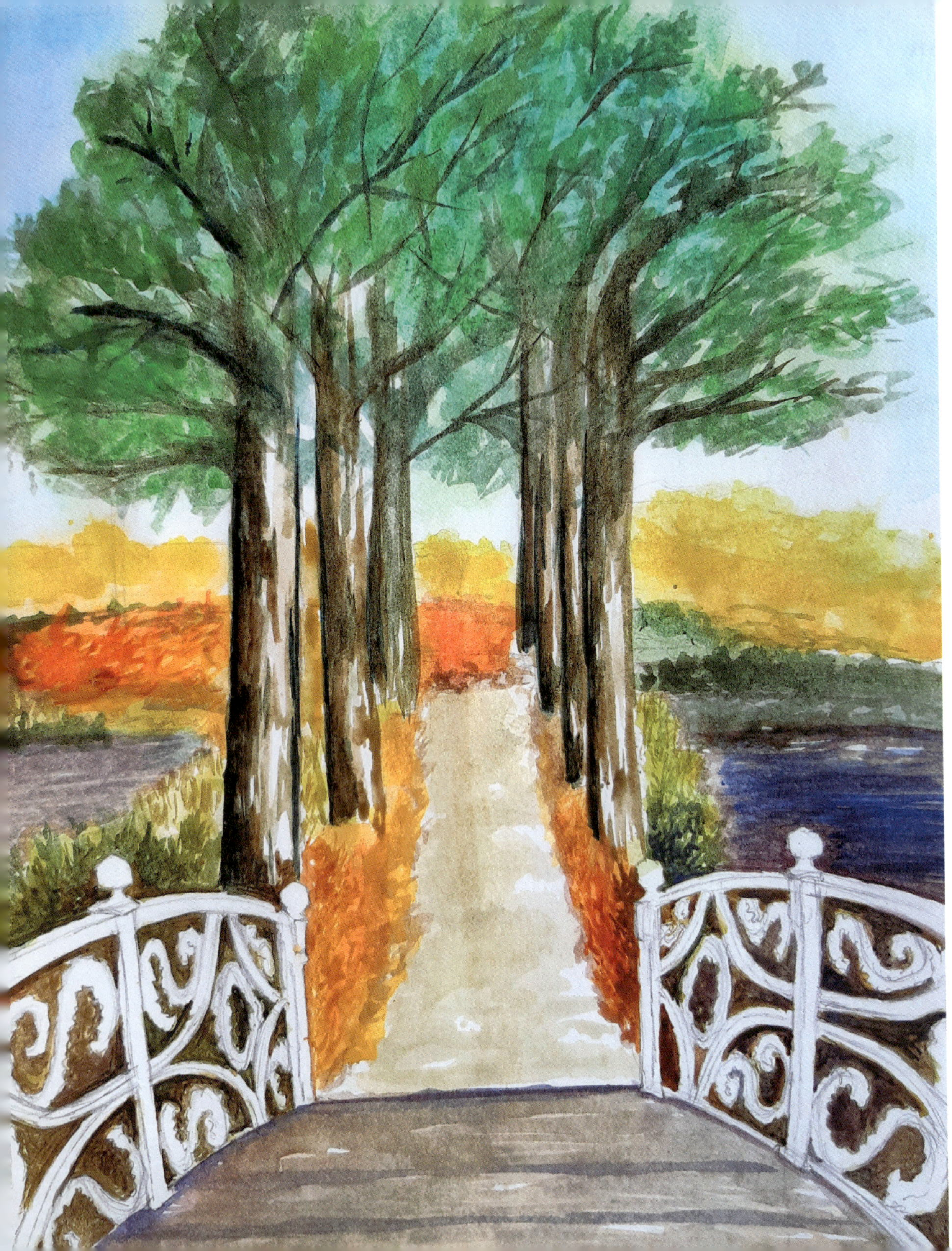

In the afternoons we used to take a stroll down the beach again. I'll mix brown, green, and white for the trail.

Nel pomeriggio avevamo l'abitudine di fare un'altra passeggiata verso la spiaggia. Mescolerò marrone, verde, e bianco per il sentiero.

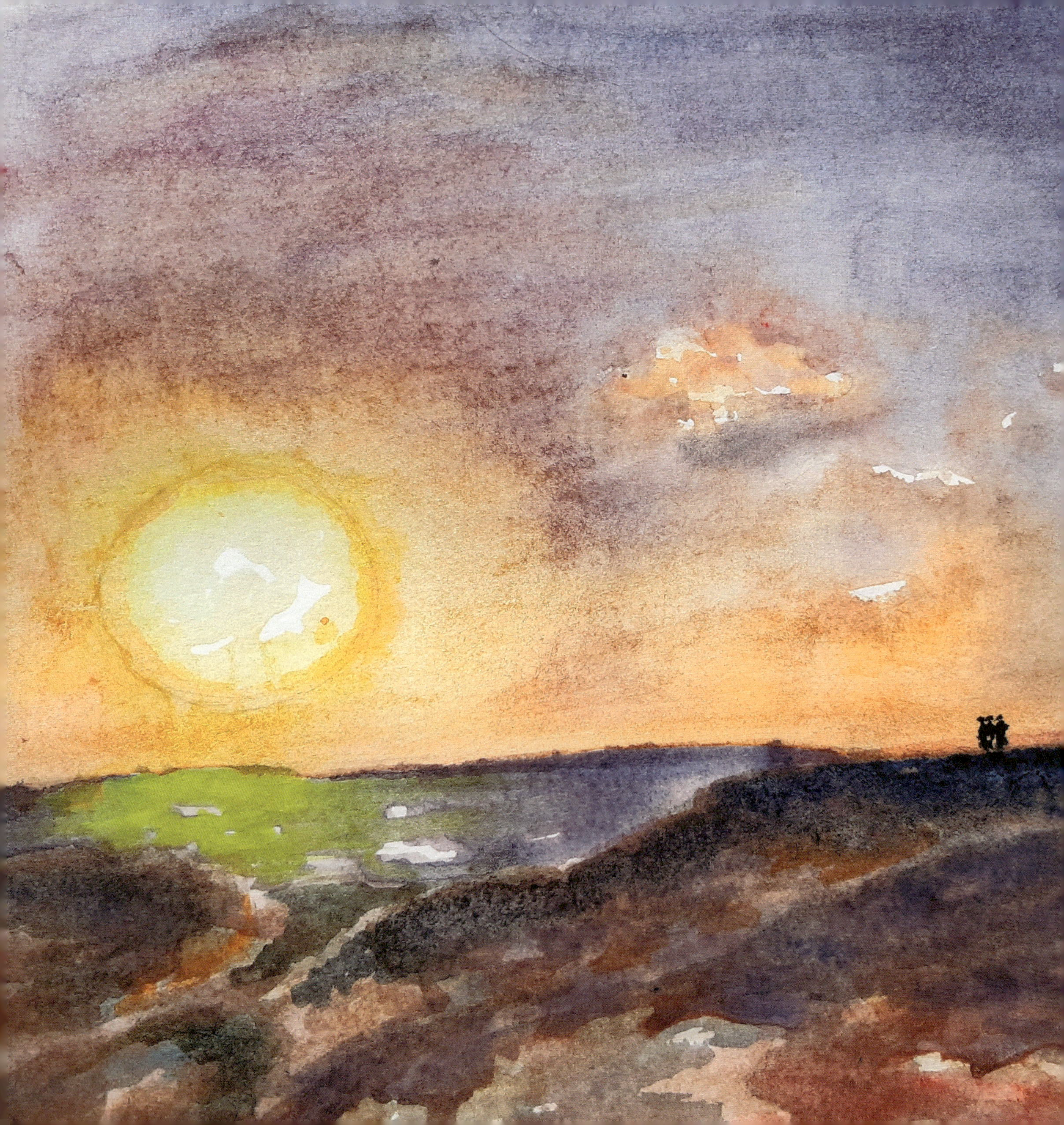

How beautiful those sunsets were!
We take a whole trip back in time with
a little purple, yellow, and brown.

Com'erano belli quei tramonti!
Facciamo un vero e proprio viaggio
indietro nel tempo con un po' di viola,
di giallo e di marrone.

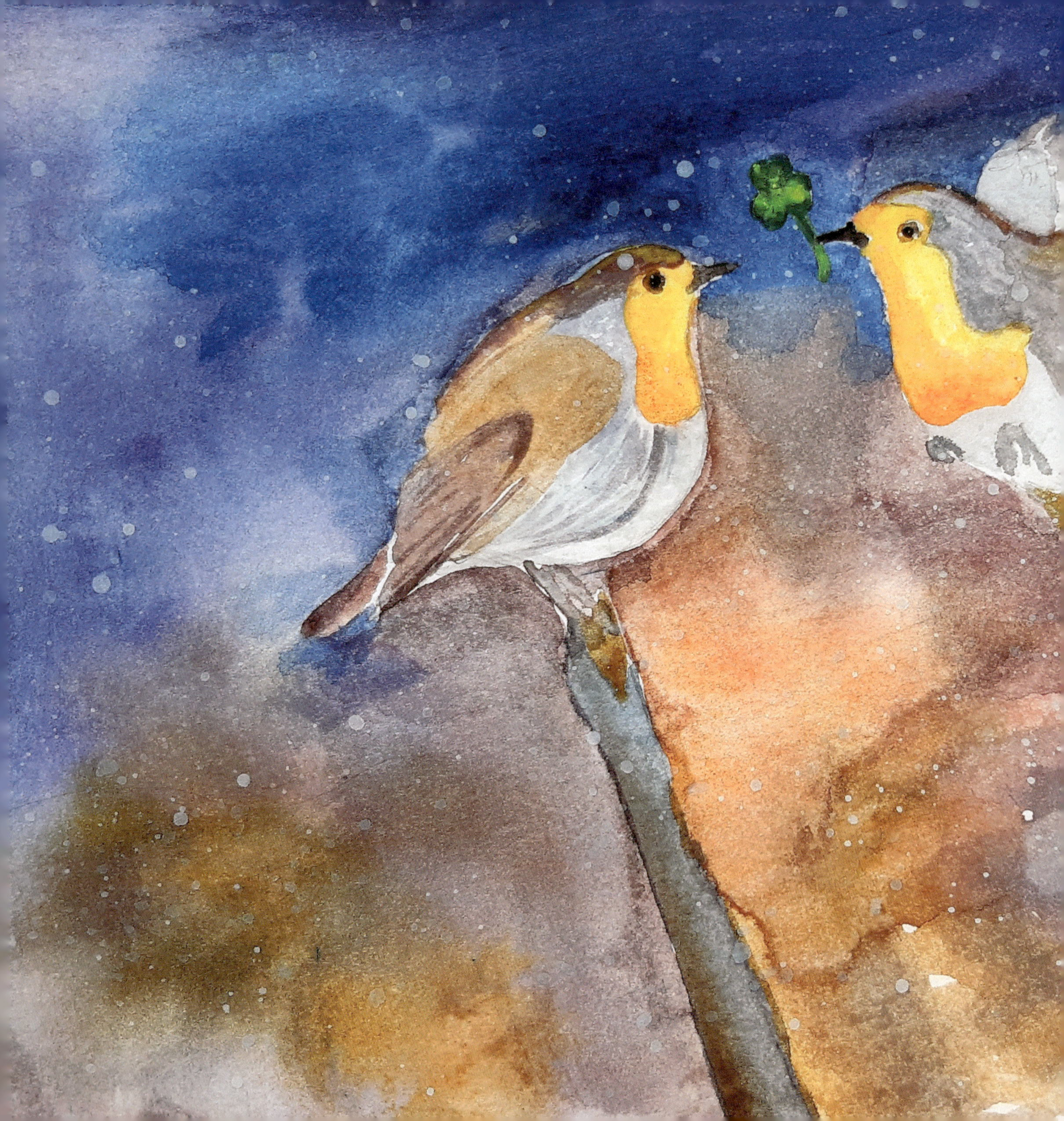

We'd bring our food with us, lay the mat down on the sand and eat under the starry sky. Dark yellow, dark blue, and a dash of red, and we're there again.

Ci portavamo qualcosa da mangiare; stendevamo la stuoia sulla sabbia, e mangiavamo sotto il cielo stellato. Giallo scuro, blu scuro e una pennellata di rosso; ed eccoci di nuovo lì.

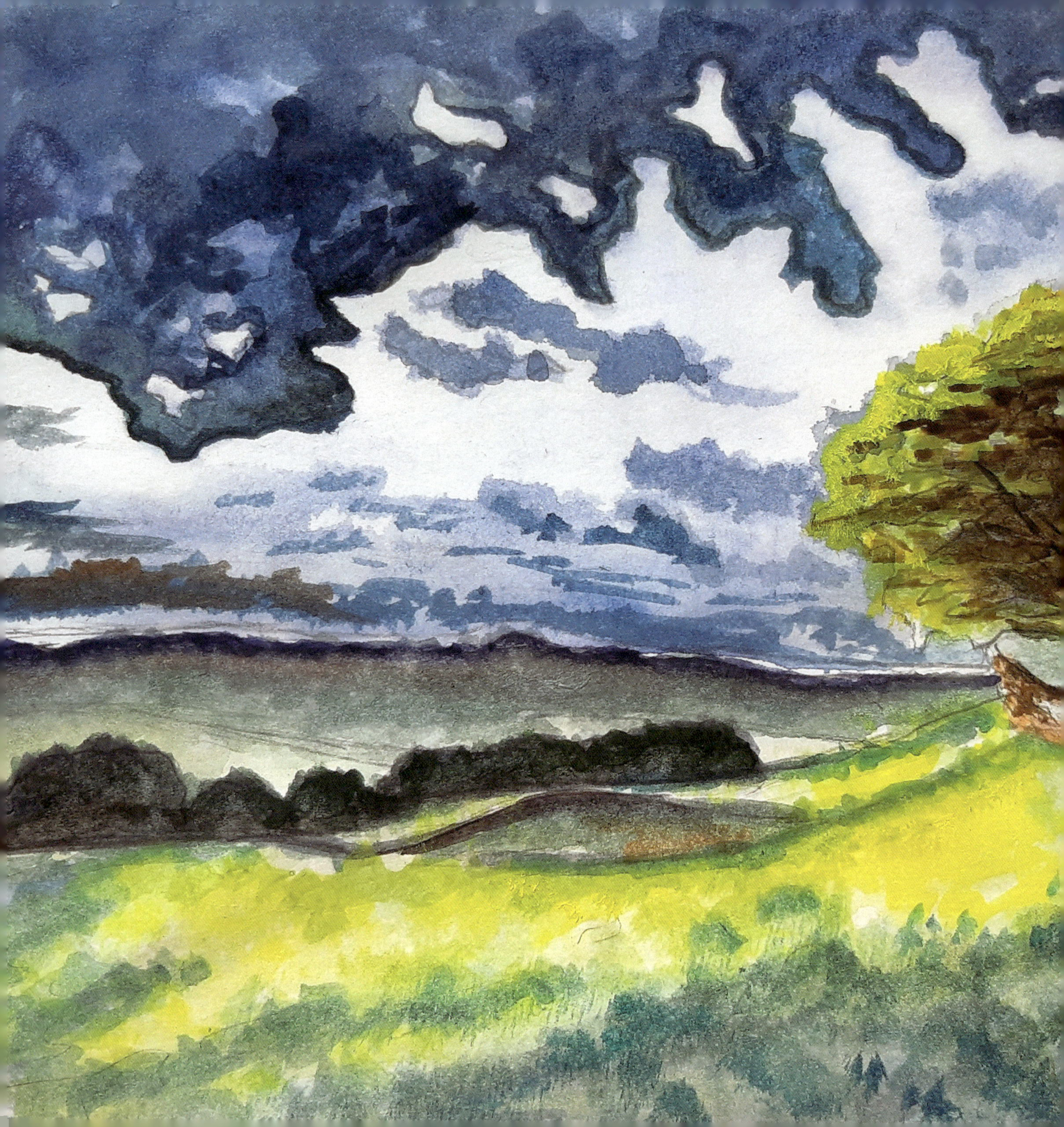

I remember the landscape
changed dramatically when
autumn came. We knew then
that it was time to leave.
Mom was coming.
The colors are getting really dark
now, intense blue, deep green.

Ricordo che il paesaggio cambiò
drammaticamente quando giunse
l'autunno. Allora capimmo che era
tempo di partire: la mamma stava
per arrivare. Ora i colori si fanno
veramente scuri: blu intenso
e verde bottiglia.

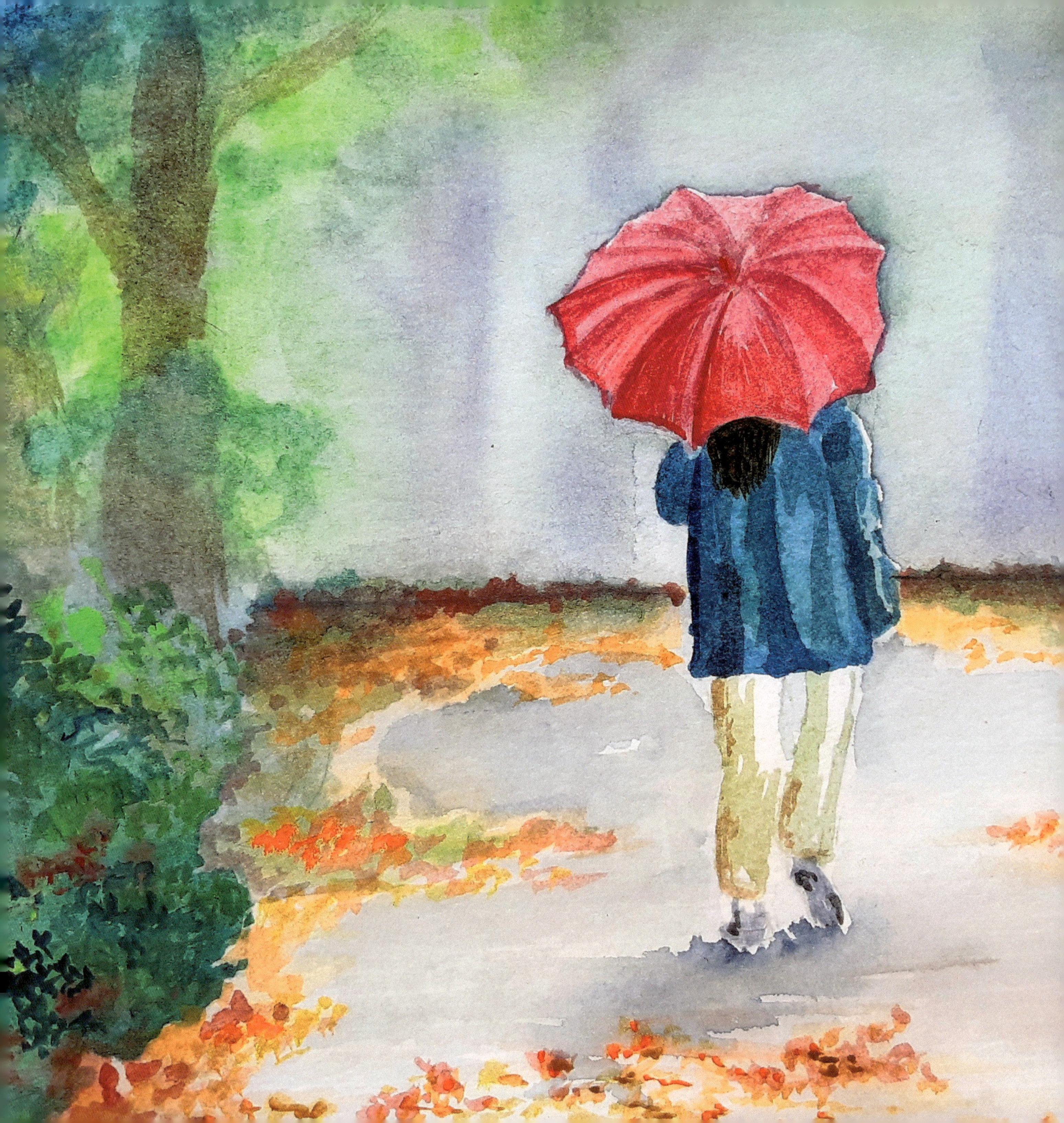

But look at the composition, how it changes again, and how the hazy colors are making room for other happier ones. Mom also brought along with her white, pink, and gold, and a promise that yes, we would leave, but we would come back again.

Ma guarda la composizione. Vedi come cambia di nuovo, come i colori cupi fanno posto ad altre tinte più allegre? La mamma infatti portò con sé bianco, rosa e oro. Ma anche una promessa: sì, saremmo partite, però saremmo tornate di nuovo.

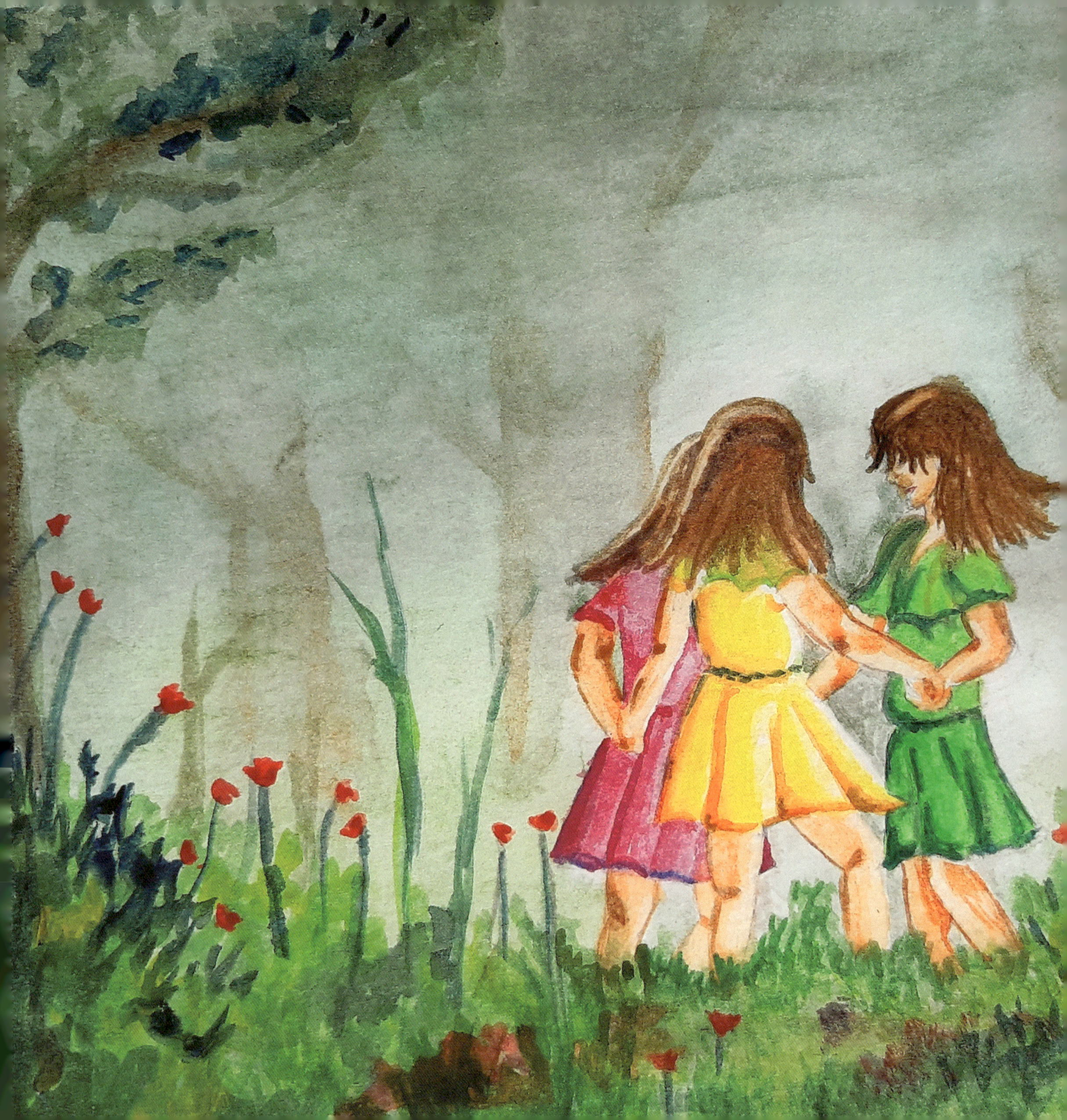

Dear Child,

Every summer has a story. This is a story inspired by my own childhood, and my sister's watercolors. Ask an adult to help you write down the words and draw the images of your own summer story, and send me an email at liza@maltamum.com I promise, I'll write back to you.

Dear Grown-up,

If you feel this book adds value to children's lives, please leave an honest review on Amazon or Goodreads.
A shout-out on social media and a tag #HappinessStreet would also be nothing short of amazing. Your review will help others discover the book and encourage me to keep on writing. Visit eepurl.com/dvnij9 for free activities, printables and more.

Forever grateful, thank you!

All my best,
Elisavet Arkolaki

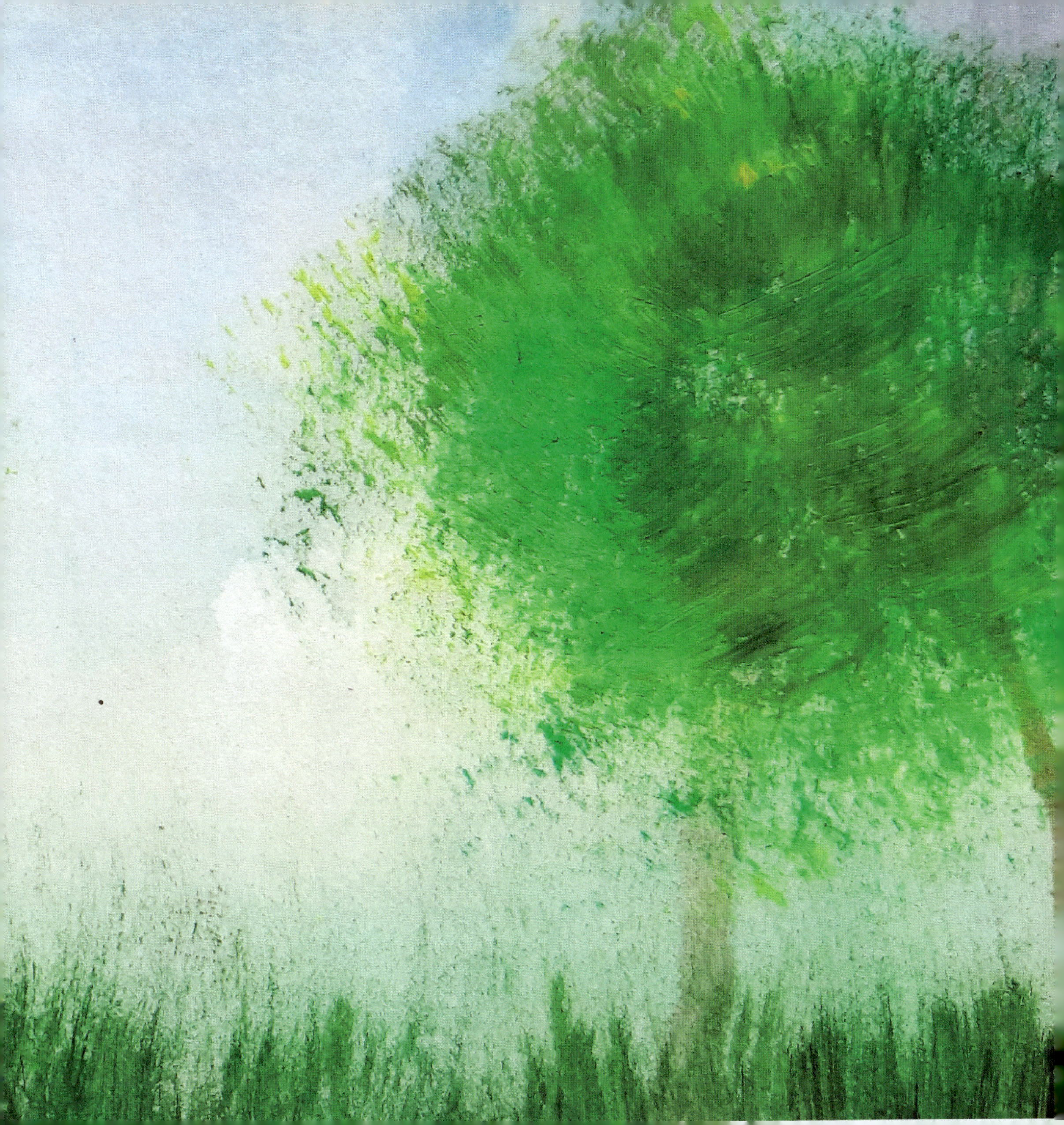

Printed in Great Britain
by Amazon